HOW TO BE FUNNY

If you purchase this book without a cover you should be aware that this book may have been stolen property and reported as "unsold and destroyed" to the publisher. In such case neither the author nor the publisher has received any payment for this "stripped book."

This is not a history book and makes no claims as such. It is a fictional story based on non-fictional events.

Published by WICKED PENZ, 2014. All rights reserved. No part of this publication may be reproduced, distributed, or transmitted in any form or by any means or stored in a database or retrieval system, without the prior written permission of the publisher.

Wicked Penz
P.O. Box 394
Sawyerville, AL 36776
(213) 255-5157

Visit our websites:
wickedpenz.com and ccomedytime.com

Printed in the United States of America

First Edition: February 2014
ISBN-13: 978-1495438653

From America's Foremost Comedy Authority

HOW TO BE FUNNY

THE ESSENTIAL COMEDY HANDBOOK

By

Darryl Littleton

TABLE OF CONTENTS

Preface	7
Dedication	12
COMEDY IS A CRAFT	14
Respect the Craft	15
The Importance of Comedy	16
Why Does Comedy Exist?	17
What makes a Person Want to do Comedy?	17
The Difference between a Comic & a Comedian	19
What Makes YOU Funny?	20
THE COMEDIAN MENTALITY	23
Comedy as Your Career	25
Mates / Family	26
Treat Comedy like A Job	26
Working a Day Job	27
Maintaining a Daily Schedule	28
How to Overcome Bitterness	29
Avoiding Complacency	30
Goal setting	31
PERFORMANCE	33
Take Your Funny Business Seriously	34
Why Do People Heckle?	35
How to Prevent Heckling	36

	Handling Hecklers	37
	Getting the Most Out Of Your Material	39
•	Research	41
•	The Formula	41
•	Stage Antics	43
•	Tags	44
•	Ad-Libbing	45
	Joke Thieves	46
	Overcoming Bombing	48
	Tape Your Shows	48
	PLAYING THE MEDIUMS	50
	Road Work	51
•	Road Decorum	51
•	Alcoholism	52
•	Ego Tripping	53
•	Violating Hotel Policies	54
	Radio	55
	TV & Film	56
•	Auditioning Techniques	56
•	On camera Techniques (maximizing time on camera)	57
	Showcases	58
	Competitions	59
•	The Ones to Enter That Can Help You	59
•	Techniques to Get Into the Winners Circle	60
	THE TOOLS OF A COMEDIAN	62
	Contracts	62
	Negotiating Techniques	67
	Obtaining Representation	70

Assembling a Motivated Team	71
Staying Relevant	71
Using Your Skills	72
IN CONCLUSION	73
Suggested Titles by the Author	76

Preface

Ever wonder why funny people win? Funny guys get the girl. Funny teachers get the awards from students.   Voters like politicians that can make them laugh. People who can bring a smile to our faces fare better in life than those who do not. We gravitate to these personalities because they make us feel good even when they're delivering bad news. Some say it's a gift, but is it?

True, there are people who are born funny. Whatever they say seems to always get a laugh.   However, that doesn't mean they know how to hone this ability. They're natural born comedians, but that isn't any guarantee that they're going to go into the field of comedy. That requires more than just being funny. Professional comedians have to have resilience, perseverance, massive egos, unmitigated gall and the unquenchable desire to show off their gift.   The fact they are funny is merely incidental, but it's also a pre-requisite for the job. The question is how really funny do you have to be to be funny enough to reap the rewards of a developed sense of humor?

All walks of life can benefit from getting laughs.

- Sales People
- Lawyers
- Politicians
- MCs
- Telemarketers
- Bail Bondsmen
- Beauticians
- Dentists
- Office Managers
- Authors / Speakers
- Newscasters
- Columnists
- Bloggers
- Clergymen
- Motivational Speakers
- Tattoo Artists
- And of course comedians

The number one fear of most people is speaking in front of an audience. It's right up there above death. That's because people fear rejection. Funny people don't share this fear. Funny people have something to say and so why would you reject them? Funny people are more afraid of dying than talking.

This handbook will teach anybody the tools to be funny. If you're a comedian the contents are indispensable. You'll not only refine an act you can take anywhere, but learn the techniques to make adjustments when needed and maximize the tools in your arsenal to brand yourself as a multi-talented performer able to work in a multitude of situations. You'll also learn the invaluable lessons of once you've attained your success, how to maintain your success.

If you're amongst the multitude of other non-comedic professions this book is your secret weapon. Your sales will increase. Your congregation will be more attentive. Your employees will be more motivated and nobody will quite know why they like you more. You'll be using the same techniques and mindset of professional laugh creators and finding how much easier your endeavors will become.

You can even use the methods in your personal life. Want to nip an impending argument in the bud? Say something funny. Need to talk your way out of a traffic ticket? Make the cop snicker. Going to the DMV? Well, not even a joke can eradicate you from that hell, but you get the drift.

Making others happier than before you showed up is the key to navigating through life with greater success. Not only will you get immediate perks; laughing gives the priceless gift of better health. Ever notice that most comedians live to be a ripe old age if they don't take themselves out? You'll look better, feel better and view the world through renewed eyes. Problems that plague the average person mean nothing to funny people because they know how to talk their way out of it. They'll get the right person to laugh.

I've been a professional comedian in a career that currently spans over four decades. Throughout my career I've worked as a stand up, comedy actor, producer of comedy, voice-over artist, author of comedy books, promoter of comedy shows, writer for over 100 comedians, interviewer for comedy documentaries, columnist for comedy magazines and I sit on the advisory board of the Comedy Hall of Fame as a comedy historian. I've helped others feed their families and attain comfortable lifestyles through the art of laughter and I'm certain these pages will assist you.

"How to Be Funny" is meant to be used as a roadmap to keep

comedians and comedy minded personalities on the right path to achieving their goals. Any person implementing these same skills can become a working professional and any working professional can gain a greater advantage. This book is here to assist in that end. Use what you're about to learn and you'll never again be without the girl, the guy, a job, friends, admirers, opportunities and the best thing of all - you'll live a happier life.

Dedication

This book is dedicated to every funny individual on the planet Earth for making this world more tolerable and habitable. Also to my late father, William Littleton Jr., who used to tell our cousins down South that we lived next door to Yul Brynner, just because they didn't know any better and couldn't prove we didn't. Dad, you were my favorite wise guy and still my only hero.

Special Thanks to my wife, Tuezdae; my daughters, Liburti and Darina; my sister, Reba; my niece, Eugena and great-nephew, Dylan; my sister-in-law, Andrea; step-daughter 'B' Brelon; and my mother, Theresa.

Normal Thanks to Duane Benjamin, Jeff Beasley and Purvis Jackson for being lifelong friends. Diaper buddies are hard to find these days.

Also thanks to Deon Cole, Guy Torry, Robert Townsend, Lauren Bailey, Greg Pittman, Doug Stanhope, Michael Ajakwe, Jr., Paul Smokey Deese, Dick Gregory, Cain Lopez, Jeff Silberman, June Clark, Brad Sanders, Arsenio Hall, Anthony Demmer, Miss Laura Hayes, Curtis Gadson, Frank

Holder, Reynaldo Rey, Robin Harris, Teddy Carpenter, Bob Sumner, Darren Fields, Lynne Harris Taylor, Rodney Winfield, Ernie G, Shang Forbes, Katt Williams, Shellee Brown, Lynn Dillard, Andre Barnwell, Benny Mena, George Perez, Buddy Lewis, Jeff Pancer, Thea Vidale, Gabriel Iglesias, E Raymond Brown, Enns Mitchell, Gary Owen, Rudy Moreno, Rushion McDonald, Terrance Reynolds, Lavell Crawford, Nikki Johnson, Eric Jerome Dickey, Emil Johnson, Spike Thompson, Doug Williams, Eddie Griffin, Franklyn Ajaye, Jamie Foxx, John Witherspoon, Marla Gibbs, Andrew Muhammad, Joey Gaynor, Michael Messina, John Cerullo, Ken Spearman, Kevin Garnier, Laverne Thompson, Loni Love, Lydia Nicole, Madd Marv, Bruce-Bruce, Gilbert Esquivel, Kenny Hill, Tom Dreesen, Howard Morris, Milton Berle, Edwin San Juan, Sebastian Cetina, Willie Barcena, D L Hughley, CJ the DJ, Vic Dunlop, Don DC Curry, Luenell Campbell, Ricco Reed, Felipe Esparza, Makena Gargannu, Daryl & Dwayne Mooney, Cedric the Entertainer, Eric Rhone, Wayne Reynolds, Sommore, David Drozen, Montanna Taylor, Tony & Rhonda Spires, Michael & Sharon Williams, Olivia Arrington, Rick Jenkins, Rodney Hardiman, Robert Keith Wyatt, Dave Chappelle, Jeff Garcia, Soni D, Colin Taylor, Joe Torry, Simply Marvelous, J. Anthony Brown and Tom Joyner for all you've taught me along my personal comedy journey.

Comedy Is a Craft

Comedy is the hardest art form. It's emotionally more difficult than music, sculpting, painting or acting because the reaction is immediate and very vocal (or not). When something funny works the receivers let the one who issued it know right away. They don't ponder the joke. They don't analyze it. They respond to it. Bam! No waiting for reviews in the paper; instant acceptance or rejection.

The general public takes comedy as a joke. Those who are good at it make it look easy and so legions of wannabes attempt grabbing the comedy brass ring annually. Every New Year's Eve a hoard of people decide they want to become comedians in one form or another. They don't swill their last vodka on the rocks before passing out and proclaim they're going to become a concert pianist in the upcoming 12 months. Nope, they're going to make a fortune telling jokes. If So & So on TV can do it why not them? What's talent got to do with it? It's the arrogance of the populace and misconception of comedy.

Accomplished comedians are craftsmen. They know the nuts and bolts of what they specialize in and make it look effortless.

They are aware of the tricks of the trade. They use their own form of study to advance their standing and proficiency. They take their art seriously.

Comedy is one of the oldest art forms known to mankind and should be treated with respect. Whether it's mime, stand-up, observational, physical, prop, improvisational or musical – all niches have their roots and pioneers. Artisans of comedy know this and honor it. If you're going to be funny consistently you should know why and how.

If comedy sees you're trying to understand its depth it can be like a good mate: it will remain loyal because you care. It may not always do as you wish, but unlike that good mate - you'll know why. Study it, appreciate it and never, ever take it for granted.

Respect the Craft

You're in the business of making people laugh. Take it seriously. All other professional fields of endeavor have a rite of passage before being deemed credible. Doctors, lawyers, scientists, chefs, all the way down to telemarketers – everybody has stuff to learn. So do comedians and just because this discipline is not mandated it has to be self-imposed. Nobody is going to hover over you or hold your hand. Comedy is a very individual and lonely art form. If you don't love it you'll drop out relatively quickly. It's not for the weak or faint of heart.

The Importance of Comedy

Comedy allows us to cope, endure and gain perspective. The first recorded writing was comedy. A comedian represents the tradition of the town crier or village wise man; that individual who was counted on to inform the others.

Laughing has proven health benefits and laughing often has been proven to provide a longer life. That should be enough, but there's more. Comedy helps you look better. Women glow and men stand taller. Taking a dip in the comedy pool is like swimming in the Fountain of Youth.

Why Does Comedy Exist?

Comedy is organic to humans. It wasn't invented. It wasn't discovered. It was simply done. From the beginning of time there was someone making everyone else laugh around the newly discovered fire.

It exists because human beings need that physical and emotional release. Could you imagine a world without laughter? Probably not. People would kill each other at a greater pace than usual.

The homosapien needs to laugh to get through things like the day, a break up or a death. We need it to relieve the tension and stress. We need it to bond with friends, family and strangers. We need comedy because the opposite is tragedy and who wants to live a life of that unless they're married to the wrong person.

What Makes a Person Want to do Comedy?

Fame!

Fortune!

Hot chicks!

Free booze!

No cost travel!

Swanky hotel suites!

Kick ass and kiss ass representation!

Fat movie deals!

Your own trailer!

Your own self-titled TV show!

A sidekick sitting next to your desk on TV to Laugh at all Your Written Jokes!

An Entourage of Parasites to Laugh at all Your Lame Jokes!

A Street or airport named after you!

Some people want to do comedy because it looks like an easy way to make a living. They're tired of their day gig and seek a glamorous way out. They're fed up with bosses, complaining co-workers and the same routine week in and week out. They want to get off their personal treadmill and run with the wind in their face. They want to be happy and all that goes along with it.

Still others get into it because they have no choice. They can't get along at so-called normal jobs because they're always cracking jokes. They can't help themselves. They have to either become comedians or stay on a first name basis with the lady at the unemployment office.

If you're compelled to say things many find humorous you're a fool to ignore that trait. Notice that when you make people laugh they're more receptive to whatever else you say? That's the magic of being funny. Chances are you're not going to get most of the things listed at the top of this section, but you will get good will and that is priceless.

People want to do comedy because it will get them good will; respect; love. And who doesn't want to be loved?

The Difference between a Comic & a Comedian

Comics tell jokes. Comedians live them. Anybody reading this book can become a comic. You learn funny material and recite it to the desired effect of getting the laugh. All phrases meticulously worked out; every word memorized. You're performing by rote meaning if somebody's head explodes in the front row you'll ignore it and go on to your next joke. You couldn't ad-lib a blister if you sat your naked behind on a hot stove. Comedians, on the other hand, can exist on stage without material. They have an act, but they don't necessarily need it. They can come up with funny situations off the top of their heads; be it the venue, the crowd, the staff, something they saw coming in the door or on the mirror in the men's room – comedians find funny everywhere without rehearsal.

There's a tendency to disrespect and shun the comic. Resist this inclination. The world needs comics. Comics entertain at county fairs, lodges, retirement parties, turn-around bus trips, etc. Comics are everywhere an audience wants just plain funny jokes. Sometimes the comic will do a well-known comedian's jokes and give them credit while telling it. Comics keep comedy going in places comedians do not tread.

Comedians work the full gamut comedy has to offer. They perform in clubs, theaters and arenas; at stadiums, on cruise ships and in casinos. They have the ability to be concert MCs, talk show hosts, game show hosts, actors, voice-overs and anything requiring a quick wit and razor sharp ad-libbing skills.

Both categories are needed in the world of comedy. For every marquee name act, dozens of accessible acts fill the bowling allies and house parties across the country. It's up to you, the reader to decide which one you're capable of becoming.

What Makes You Funny?

What *does* make you funny? When people laugh at you – why? Do you make funny faces? Do you have a funny voice? Are you a great story teller? Do you contort your body and do physical antics? Or do you do impressions?

Whatever it is that attracts people to your sense of humor is what should be used as a comedian. Chances are the greatest laughs you've ever produced were spontaneous with friends or out in the public. You didn't plan it. It wasn't part of an act. You just saw an opportunity to be funny and you seized it, but what drove that laughter?

Unfortunately a lot of comics talk about things that have nothing to do with how they want to be perceived. Not you. You want an act that brands you and makes it easy for the public to remember you. So once we identify what makes you funny that strength can be used to make a good comedian. First you have to figure out how you're perceived.

There are 3 levels of perception:

1. How you see you
2. How you think people see you
3. How people actually see you

It's a waste of everyone's time if you get on stage thinking you're sexy, but the audience sees a slob. You should be getting standing ovations with slob jokes and not bombing with sexy jokes. The point is not to glorify yourself, but to win over your audience.

There's an old saying, "You can look good and lose or look bad and win." Very few successful comedians throughout history came off as cool while doing their comedy, but when you saw them in candid pictures they all looked cool. They knew how to play the game. And our game is to entertain, not to be the coolest person in the room. Save your cool for your circle of family and friends. Success is very cool.

The Comedian Mentality

If you're aware of the realities of a situation, you're better equipped to handle them. As previously stated comedy is the hardest of all the arts. In music a mediocre band can play a popular song and muddle through. You can go to a museum and look at paintings and sculptures and debate their merits with other patrons who might have other interpretations of their meaning. A work of literature comes alive differently for whoever is the reader. Acting and dancing are also subjective. But comedy gets an immediate response from a group that cannot be ignored. If nobody laughs at a joke it is deemed not funny and the comedian failed.

I say that to say as a comedian you will bomb. All the greats did it. You will too. The goal is to do it as little as possible and to not happen when the stakes are high; such as an industry showcase or a national television appearance. There are tricks to avoid bombing or at least to minimize its affects.

Another reality is public adulation. You can't take your career personally. You're a public figure; a commodity. You need to understand that the public does not know you and will treat you as an object. Historically the crowd looks for something new. When they find it they embrace it and sometimes overrate it. Either way, they eventually tire of it and seek out the newer new. The old thing they once loved now suffers a backlash; meaning it's time to reinvent or retire. As long as you understand this you can avoid being bitter and harboring feelings of being unwanted or unappreciated. You'll always have value as a human being, but as a talent your usefulness is in flux.

Not everybody wants to be a star. Some comedians simply want to make a living making people laugh. Well, comedy offers many options to making a solid living. The key - knowing who you are and what will make you happy in this profession.

Do you like to travel?	Become a road comic.
Are you a leader?	Focus on producing or directing.
Are you a follower?	Try comedy acting.
Do you like to be alone?	Think about being a writer.
Are you shy?	Look into being a ventriloquist.

Comedy as Your Career

There's an awful lot to learn about comedy and the education never ends. So you have to be certain that life as a comedian is what you really want. You can't be wishy-washy about it. It won't let you.

Comedy feels it's offering too much for you to resist. If you can get past the fact you just might not be a mega-star, as a comedian you possess a number of talents that can be marketed. Some will become writers, producers, directors, club owners, managers, agents, promoters, bloggers, columnists, commentators and various other off-shots of comedy. Comedians that stay behind the mic might wind up on cruise ships, doing voice-overs, acting, hosting all kinds of events, doing radio, a game show or a talk show.

In other words you signed up to be funny. There's a lot of ways to do it so don't be a snob.

Mates / Family

Don't expect your family to support your comedy aspirations. They'll think it's cute. They'll encourage you then in the same breath tell you they can get you a job where they work if you're interested. They know you're going to be a big time comedian actor one day, but in the meanwhile . . .

Your friends will be a little more sympathetic. They're actually hoping you make it so they can get in on the good times. There are stars they want to meet and they figure you'll be able to make the introductions. Then reality sets in when you're not a household name six months after you got in comedy. Now they're giving you jokes to help your little act.

Don't worry - when you become successful that will all change. That's part of the reason you stay the course.

Treat Comedy like It's a Job

A so-called "real" job has a schedule. It's got a start time, breaks, a lunch and an end time. If comedy and being funny is your "real" job you have to have such a schedule. Your day is comedy, not just waiting for night time so you can hit the clubs. Oh that's right – I forgot to mention a "real" job has a real boss; somebody to whom you have to be accountable. Well, in your career that's you. Ultimately you are your own boss. How do you feel about the way you're running things?

If you were to make a productivity chart and have some graphs would the company known as 'you' be doing well? Are you a thriving corporation or are you barely hanging on; hoping for a miracle. No matter who else is on your staff (agent, manager, publicist) you are at the helm. Everybody is working "for" you. However, they will stop if you're not working. So work and do it better than for any other employer you ever had. Why not? This one knows your mama.

Working a Day Job

You've got to eat, don't you? Nobody objects to a comedian having a day job as long as it's not a day career. If you're trying to get a gold watch from the place maybe that's your destiny and not the humor industry. If you're doing it to keep food on the table while your comedy moves are panning out then that's the point. An artist literally starving is a funky, cranky, desperate artist. So please eat so you don't rob me.

Maintaining a Daily Schedule

Most professions have a routine. Comedians should as well. Your day needs to consist of advancing to another phase. You need to come up with something new every day. The fact is as a funny person you are a creator. You take nothing and put something in its place. Do that every day. Practice your act. Write new material. Read something to expand your knowledge and insight. Work on your goals. Set new goals.

Your daily schedule will depend on what's going on in your career at the time. If you're shooting a film or broadcast show your schedule will revolve around that (even though there is still time to slip in a new joke to your collection). If you're touring there is always time to add to your future. Don't make the mistake of coasting just because you're working. Movies wrap and shows get cancelled. Being funny is your cushion. Once one project ends you can go to the next because you're good.

When you're not working is the real time to devote to your daily schedule. What you do today will have profound effects on what happens tomorrow, next week or the following year. Being successfully funny is a 24/7/365 proposition. You're always on call. So there – you've been warned.

How to Overcome Bitterness

Bitterness sets in when expectations are not met. It's usually an affliction for veteran comedians (anything over 10 years in the game). They had dreams and for one reason or another haven't lived them. Yet they've watched many of their peers get over, get rich and become the names friends and family bring up when discussing comedy and not you. Hell, they're surprised you even know that person.

If you're bitter because your road was different than your peers you need to ask yourself why. Have you worked as hard as your peers? Were you more trouble than you were worth when you were working? Be honest with yourself. It's not a pop quiz later, no need to cheat. This is your career and at very least – your time.

There comes a period when reinvention might be the key. If you're a veteran comedian odds are the industry has seen you. They know who you are and feel they also know what you're capable of doing. The industry is often wrong; proven so by so many artists who altered that perception by reinvention. The industry strives on what's new. Acts are like jokes – once you've heard it you know it. Surprise me.

Success comes in waves. Perhaps your peers caught the wave you missed. Another one is coming. Get on that one, but not with the same tools. Give them another side of you. Show them you're not a one trick pony. If you want to overcome being bitter – get rid of the person you feel got passed over and explore the new one that won't.

Reinvention could mean anything from crafting a new act where you incorporate your other skills (singing, playing a musical instrument, etc.) to moving behind the scenes as a writer, director or producer. It could mean concentrating on acting as opposed to stand-up. Ever think about going into radio? The options are there to be tried. Trust me; bitterness will be waiting for you if everything else fails.

Avoiding Complacency

The best way to avoid complacency is to keep your desire in comedy alive. If you find yourself on the treadmill and the routine is wearing you down – take time off. Take as much as you need. Take so much time off that you're aching to go back up. Then take off even more time, but still go to comedy clubs. Watch the other comedians. Observe your peers get better and grow as you're taking time off. Imagine them getting their own TV shows or movie deals while you're still on the sidelines. Then get back on stage and into the race . . . or not.

If you don't care about relinquishing your slot to others then remain at or get a day job. Comedy is not for you anyway. A funny person can't feel whole without being funny and the thought of other funny people outshining them brings out their competitive spirit. You may not want to be the top comedian, but you'll be damned if you don't feel you could be.

Another way to avoid complacency is . . . .

Goal setting

All careers set goals. Comedy is no different. Achievements are measured by the attaining of these goals. You've decided to be funny in one aspect or another. You also need to set goals. Set daily goals such as time devoted to your practicing your material or spent writing material. There should be weekly goals, monthly goals, seasonal, annual and goals than extend 5 years, 10 years and throughout your career.

How do you want to be remembered? If they give you a lifetime achievement award what do you want them to say? What clips do you want to see? What legacy do you want to leave? What you accomplish now will determine how your career is viewed. Take it seriously now or look back later with regret.

Performance

How do you describe your comedy persona in a single phrase?

If *you* can't do it chances are nobody else can either. That means you have no brand. Everything should have a brand. You grew up on branded products: McDonald's, Pepsi, Doritos, Roscoe's, Nike, Pantene, Kellogg's, Microsoft and so on.

Entertainers have brands too. When you think about Lisa Lampanelli you get a certain image. If you were casting a film about girls on a road trip seeking men would you cast her or not? Or would you cast Ellen?

Here are some examples of branding:

When you think Tim Allen you think tools
Roseanne = domestic housewife
Arnez J = physical comedy
Jerry Seinfeld = observational comedy
Corey Holcomb = comedy blasting women
T K Kirkland = comedy about oral sex
Bill Cosby = family comedy
Bill Maher = political comedy (liberal)

Dennis Miller = political comedy (conservative)

Paul Mooney = racial comedy

All of these individuals have a brand. Cedric tells you his brand in his name, Cedric the Entertainer. Another method of branding is to say your name throughout your act or your POV (point of view).

The point of branding is to let the public know they're getting something familiar; something they already know that they either like or don't. However, within that brand, you, the artist surprise them with how you present the familiar. Sure James Bond will always defeat the villain; the question is how.

Branding separates you from the pack and makes it easier for promoters to book you to specific audiences. The goal is to pick your spots. True, you want to be able to play to any audience, but the reality is not all audiences will be your fans. You want to get in front of people that will support you career as long as you choose to have one.

Take Your Funny Business Seriously

In comedy there are no victims, only volunteers. Nobody forced you to do anything. So if you're going to do it, do it like you mean it. Don't play around. Study, learn, apply, grow, explore, expand, collaborate, mentor, speak, reminisce and be the recipient. Making people laugh is a great way to make a living. The perks are good, but comedy also makes you feel good.

However, before you start feeling too good, I'm sure there are a few questions you might want answered. For instance...

Why Do People Heckle?

When you're funny there's always somebody out there who thinks they're funnier. Like gunslingers in the Old West they're gonna come a gunnin' for ya. You're on a show. You're the center of attention. The heckler might not have come to heckle, but now that they're there it's going down. They are funnier than you and they're going to prove it.

Comedians don't heckle other comedians. It's an unwritten rule. However, we do enjoy seeing it go down. We can't wait to check out how or if the comedian will get out of it. Since the vast majority of hecklers have been drinking you'd think it would be easy to out think them and it is. The problem is they think they're making sense and won't shut up.   Security!

How to Prevent Heckling

The best sure fire way to prevent heckling is to be so funny nobody can hear the heckler over all the laughing. Hecklers can only heckle when there's a gap in the action. They don't yell over a set up or scream at you during the punchline. Hecklers only attack when there's silence. It doesn't have to be a lot; a millisecond is really all most need, but in that time they will blurt out.

Hecklers will also blurt out if they feel you're vulnerable. A good way to show confidence, even if you're shaking like a leaf is to pace; stalk the stage like a caged animal. Hecklers don't care for constant motion. They also don't like direct eye contact. So try to scan everybody's eyes. That really throws hecklers off; moving and looking. At any moment you might zero in on them and initiate the attack.

In either case, destroy the heckler's hopes and dreams of conquest at your expense – quickly! As soon as they open their mouth to say anything but "Bravo" let in on them with a solid line that would put most in their place. If they persist have a barrage at the ready and use them. Don't let the heckler get a word in edgewise as you pepper them relentlessly with great vengeance and furious anger.

Handling Hecklers

You should have at least a half-dozen heckler lines in your back pocket. Even if you're "not that type of comedian" you might have to temporarily morph into that type if the going gets too rough and you need to defend yourself. Dirty comic, clean comic – doesn't matter. Every comic needs to know a patron can't walk in the door and get the best of them.

Sometimes hecklers are drunks getting too loud. This is technically not heckling as much as an annoying distraction. Fire a warning shot. "Damn, where did you folks learn to whisper – in a helicopter?" By simply acknowledging the volume the table in question will quiet down and you can go on with your act. If not you can get them.

Sometimes hecklers are there to heckle. Waste no time in getting them. Hit them hard and hit them with malice. They came to mess up your show. It is personal. It's you against them. Win. You have the mic. You have the attention of the audience. How dare somebody try to come to your job and make you look bad? Intentional hecklers are your enemy. Treat them accordingly.

If you can't destroy them with targeted ad-libs get them with stand-by standards. There are many books on snapping you can get. They will give you more than ample ammo for these situations. In the meanwhile here are a few examples using your dear beloved mother to drive home the point:

"Yo mama is so fat the back of her neck looks like a pack of hot links."

"Your mama is so stupid she tried to line up M & M's in alphabetical order."

"Yo mama's got so many crabs she walks sideways."

"Yo mama has a wooden leg and a real foot."

"Yo mama has a suede tittie."

"Yo mama gives so much head she thinks it's natural to walk on her knees."

Hecklers should not be tolerated. However, if all fails and the heckler is getting off on being attacked (which is known to happen for those who only heckled to get attention for themselves) use your last resort and say, "Security". Don't cry it like you need help. Don't say it like you're angry. Say it as though the audience has had enough and you're trying to spare them another moment of having their time wasted. The subtext is they came to see you (or a comedy show) and the heckler has now made you have to assure they get what they came for and they didn't come to hear that person. Act heroic.

Getting the Most Out Of Your Material

You want to know how to be funny?

Say the first thing that pops into your head. No filtering. No editing. Just say it. 99% of the time that will be the funniest version.

Comedy is the element of surprise. That very first thought surprised you, right? You didn't see it coming. Whereas, those latter incarnations lack the thrust of going from the unknown to the known. Blurt it out no matter how inappropriate. Blurt it out no matter how taboo. Blurt it out unless it's going to get you killed instantly. Trust the blurt. It will serve you well.

Anybody can get a laugh. You're trying to be funny. If you're in touch with your attitudes about things don't suppress them. You're being funny for other human beings who either share your plight or know somebody who did/does.

So be fearless. What are you really afraid of: that a group of imperfect strangers will reject your imagination and utter the sound, "boo"? Nobody is going to throw you behind bars or kill you. So if brief rejection is the worst case scenario, why not go out guns blazing? Have no fear. A large percentage of people find that funny.

Confidence is 90% of being funny. Never back off of your jokes. You said them for a reason. Don't let some lackadaisical audience sway your core beliefs (stage beliefs that is). Deliver your material like you're buying everything you're selling. You don't have to be liked, just in control and of course, funny.

Comedy is supposed to be said like you're talking to your best friend. It should be intimate yet be energetic. Audiences like ad-libs because they know they are spontaneous. The true ability to be funny in any circumstance is to create the illusion of spontaneity even though what is being said has been said before. Living in the moment is a key to swaying an individual or group to see things your way; your funny way.

It also helps if you smile. Not a big stupid grin. Not a subservient cheesy grin. Present a genuine smile that is warming, comforting and reassuring. It allows an audience to relax. They feel at ease with you and it appears as though you're having a good time. A smile also causes people to lower their defenses. Smile and you can damn near say

anything to anybody and get away with it - on or off stage.
However, when you're on stage no amount of smiling will get
you over if you're not saying anything funny.

Here's the key components you'll need to know:

- **Research**

    You never want to put a foot in your mouth with a mic in your
    hand. You should always know what you're talking about when
    you're in front of an audience. If you don't *you* become the
    joke. On bits that go beyond the knowledge already in your
    head – research it. Get your facts straight.

- **The Formula**

    The best bits waste no words. Get to the point. Every word
    drives the next.

    People laugh at dialogue, but they also laugh at rhythm;
    cadence. A baby who cannot speak will laugh at a joke they
    do not understand if the rhythm is correct.

    The basic formula for a joke is Set Up >>>>>Punchline. Tell
    us what you're talking about then hit us with a surprise ending.

    The Set Up can be a statement.

Example Set Up: "My cousin Jimmy is real country."
Punchline – "If I had a nickel for every tooth he had in his mouth I'd have a nickel."

Or the Set Up could be a question answered by a question.
Example Set Up: "Ladies, is it sexy when a man walks around with his gut hanging out?"
Punchline: "Then why do you think it is when you do it?"

Or the Set Up could be a question answered by a statement.
Example Set Up: "Why'd the chicken cross the road?"
Punchline: "Because there were some black guys coming at him with a skillet of hot grease."

In any case the Punchline has to be the payoff and for that to work the payoff word has to be the last thing we hear.

If I say, "Women like their men tall. A girl said to me, 'I like to look up to my man' so I said, 'Good, get on your knees then."

That's not nearly as funny as if I'd said . . . .
"Women like their men tall. A girl said to me 'I like to look up to my man' so I said, 'Good, then get on your knees."

The surprise word in that example is "knees". The joke doesn't work without that visual. It has to be the last thing we hear, not "then" said after it. Nothing should ever be said after the punch word. Ever notice how some jokes said end with, "and shit"?

Example "That dude was so ugly he made little kids run in the house *and shit*."

The "and shit" is there because rhythmically the joke doesn't work. The punch word isn't strong enough to end the joke right there.

- **Stage Antics**

    Whatever you do on stage that is non-verbal should still be under the umbrella of comedy and/or entertainment.

- If you're going to go on stage dancing before telling a single joke, that dance should either be:

A) Funny OR
B) Dazzling – a dance few people in the room can do.

    Other than that you're merely killing time and squandering the good will of the audience.

- If you're going to bring a member of the audience on stage for a bit that interaction needs to be funny. That means you have some idea where it's going before it takes place. Don't let your volunteer actually control your routine (it should only appear that way).

- If you use music in your routine and have to rely on a DJ you never met before in life – STOP DOING THAT ROUTINE!

As a performer you never want to put your act in the hands of a disinterested party. If you didn't pay your new partner, the DJ will forget your cue, miscue your cue or be outside smoking a cigarette or in the bathroom when your cue comes up. Now you have to tell your audience that the DJ messed up your joke. Unless that was part of your gag it sounds very unprofessional. Your act is derailed and now you have to adlib your way out of it.

- **Tags**

Tags are like aftershocks. They reverberate. Tags are little punchlines you can say after the punchline to add more oomph to a joke.

Example: "The guy was so black he got arrested for riding around with tinted windows."

Tag # 1 – in a convertible

Tag #2 – wearing shades

Tag #3 – in broad daylight

In comedy there's a thing known as "The Rule of 3". It's the belief that a bit can be tagged three times and then the comedian should move on to the next bit. This rule was meant to be broken. One of the old gag men from the Sid Caesar's classic, "Show of Shows", Howard Morris once told me they would tag bits not only three times, but 33 times if the audience was still laughing.

That requires great proficiency in the next section which is . . .

- **Ad-Libbing**

Ad-libbing is the art of spontaneity. It's the ability to be verbally free; not restricted by social conventions. You're talking out of the box of your act. It's the purest and most naked form of you on stage because not even you know what's going to happen next. It's an exciting time. You're ignoring the safety net known as your act.

Your act should be like balloons floating above your head. They're always there when you need them and should only be used if you need them. As a funny person you should be able to walk on any stage and just say funny things off the top of your head. When you run out of spontaneous funny things, grab one of your balloons and pop it.

You should never be at a loss because you have so many things to ad-lib about: the venue, the staff, the promoter, the people in the front row, the people too scared or cheap to be in the front row, the town, the lack of whatever the town lacks, what happened to you that day, your hotel accommodations, the person that has too much to drink and now they're getting loud, the person who brought the lush to the venue, the temperature in the room, and so on and so on. There is an endless array of things to discuss; from how you feel to what you think.

Ad-libbing is a muscle you should work on every time you get on stage (unless it's a TV taping. Save experimentation for the gym, not fight night)

Joke Thieves

These individuals are low. No doubt about it. A joke thief is in comedy for all the wrong reasons (too many to list). The best thing a professionally minded comedian can do is steer clear of these colleagues (no matter how good natured they will steal from you one day as well) and nobody is above suspicion.

Your friends in comedy will steal from you. Your enemies in comedy will steal from you. People who don't even know they're stealing from you will steal from you. Once a joke has been said anybody can steal from you. Some don't know it's wrong to pilfer the labor of another when it comes to jokes. Others don't care. It's been said that the joke belongs to the comic that gets it on TV first.

A joke truly belongs to the person who wrote it. That's fact, which has nothing to do with application. Thieves will come. Your job is to keep writing. If you're married to jokes – your supply will soon be depleted. You must continue to grow as a comedian.

The other course of action is to beat a joke thief showing no mercy. Send the signal out to one and all that you don't play that. You can wield a bat or hire thugs to administer the ass whooping. You can slit tires. You can bust windshields. There's a lot of violent things you can do. Or you can call them out right while they're on stage saying your stolen joke. Watch them turn colors and start sweating. Then listen to them deny it with an audience as witnesses. Good times to be had by all.

Overcoming Bombing

You're bound to bomb. Some will bomb so bad they'll wallow in depression. They'll question their funny; if they really are funny at all. When that happens analyze the set. Figure out what went wrong and how you can handle the next time something like that happens again (and it will. Bad experiences in comedy always repeat themselves) and then shake it off by pulling out and viewing some of your successful performances.

Comedy is not baseball. In baseball a player can strike out 7 out of 10 times and still be considered a good player with a batting average of .300. If a comedian bombs 7 out of 10 times it's time to consider another line of work – you stink.

So put your little bomb in perspective. It's going to happen and few are career enders. So get over it and go kill them on the next show!

Tape Your Shows

Taping your sets is invaluable. It helps you build material as well as eliminate the jokes you have that simply don't work. I suggest a small digital recorder. Once your set is over, listen to it on the drive home. Be critical. Take notes when you get home. If you ad-libbed something funny that can be used again – add it to the act. Without that recording you might've forgotten it all together. Break each set down and make the appropriate changes. It's your act. Who do you trust more than yourself to get it where you want it to go? So be the best boss you ever had and get the results you want. You know how to communicate with you better than anyone. So get it done.

Playing the Mediums

It doesn't matter how funny you are if you don't have a platform to present it. You can crack yourself up in front of the mirror all day. Who cares? You need a place to be seen or heard. There are a number of options to choose from so don't limit your ambitions, but also don't go into any of them without understanding the rules of those mediums.

Stand-up comedy is the most direct way to reach an audience. It is the freest art form in the sense of individual expression. It's just you, the microphone and your imagination. Nobody is going to edit what you say. Nobody can make you look better or worse than what you present.

It's actually the only time in comedy you will have that freedom. In film and television much of what a comic will say will be scripted. In stand up you write the script and so you have to deal with the backlash of a bad one. You're completely responsible for what comes out of your mouth and I'm sure you don't want to get hit in it for saying the wrong thing; on or off stage. That's why the medium of live performance is more than what you do during your show. It encompasses your behavior before and after as well.

Road Work

The road is the best and worst place to work. It carries wonders and mysteries. It also carries a lot of danger. Attack it like a professional and you should be okay. Hop into any car because dude has weed and chicks back at his house and you might be in the next memorandum.

Here's some tips for working far from home and returning.

Road Decorum

Not every place on the road is the same. Since you don't want to go to jail and not make the gig; know the laws of where you're going. If weed is frowned upon, don't have any weed. Drive slow and easy. Obey all posted signs. The road can be very unforgiving. Don't let it get you by dropping your guard. You're not the first comedian traveling through town. There are con artists, pimps, distraction girls and assorted scams await you. Do your job and you can avoid most. Act like people you just met are really your new friends and you might never see your old ones again. Not trying to scare you – just saying.

Alcoholism

The booze is free. Who's not going to abuse that? Professionals. Drinking is so prevalent in comedy a lot of comedians don't realize they're alcoholics even though they drink 2-3 drinks a night 5-6 nights a week. It's taken for granted and easy to do. One drink before you hit the stage; maybe one while you're on stage and a drink or two when you get off. You're a drunk. You think you rocked, but your antics amused the audience. You being loaded *was* the joke, not your jokes. You're used to this type of drinking so you might not slur your words or stagger to your car, but your liver hates your guts.

Regardless of your tolerance level the problem is drinking becomes a crutch. Instead of being able to take it or leave it, you have to have a drink to do your act. For some comedians it's a specific type or brand. For others any old swill will do. Either way when it gets to that point your drinking becomes more important than the show. Fine for you, but you're not being paid to drink up your free liquor and bomb. The word will get out and you'll get put on that list; the promoter's alcoholic ledger. Your work will dry up quicker than your shot glass.

Free liquor is a perk, not a tool. If you feel like a kid in a candy store, act like you're allergic. Your career will thank you.

Ego Tripping

When you go from being anonymous to a recognized commodity your ego takes that journey with you. You don't have to be a star. It's enough that you were that person on stage. You were the one being funny. While you were up there people actually wanted to be you or lay you. A person has to be a lot more than level headed not to let it go to your head. Girls that wouldn't give a funny guy the time of day are now asking you to come by. People are treating you special. When you're a comedian you get a lot of free stuff: T-Shirts, caps, weed, etc. Then you get ass kissers; people that go overboard in their adulation of you.

Control you ego. Yes, most people will put their butts upon their shoulders and act like their fecal matter is fragrant – for a while. Shooting to the stratosphere is expected, but you're also expected to level off and return to the planet Earth. Most folks will allow that progression, but when the ego prolongs that period or goes haywire, then you're dubbed an asshole.

Nobody wants to be bothered with you and though you may be funny – you're not so funny they have to deal with you. Fortunately there are other comedians on the planet. We'll just get somebody else, asshole.

Violating Hotel Policies

The fact is you can be banned from hotels and their various chains. Peeing in the pool, sexually harassing the staff, streaking or any other policy breakers are reasons for the hotel to kick you out and the promoter who got you the room to put out the word about you and not book you again. They also have the right to terminate you from the gig without pay.

There are fees that go along with violations. If you smoke in a non-smoking room there's a fee. Steal a robe and get caught – that cost. They feel the same way if you steal a TV too. So the best course of action is to use the room for what rooms are normally used for, check out on time and don't forget to leave a tip for housekeeping on the pillow.

Needless to say, this information applies to hotel lodging that's bought for you. If you're paying for the room yourself you can pretty much do what the hell you want.

Radio

Radio is known as the theater of the mind. It's the place where the listener's imagination is only limited by your visual input. You control what they see by what you say. The great comedians from the past gained tremendous joke delivery strength from working radio. You can too.

When you're on radio remember silence is your enemy. You've got to keep the chatter going no matter what. If a listener turns to your station and it's quiet – they keep turning. Also keep in mind the chatter they do hear has to be funny. You're not a song you're a comedian. Your job is not to have people tapping their feet, but laughing. If you're advertising an upcoming show and you're not funny on radio don't expect a packed house. You weren't funny on radio.

The best way to be funny on radio is to have set gags. Have the DJ set you up then deliver the goods. From there you want to be spontaneous yet calculated. Use the wall of sound technique. This requires you to keep running funny lines from the time you're introduced until they bid you farewell. Think anarchy and chaos. You want the DJ to practically kick you out of the booth you've taken over so much. What do you have to lose? You're not working at the DJs club. Be funny.

TV & Film

Working in the mediums in front of the camera is the goal of most comedians. We love the stage, but the ultimate is the silver or small screen. Getting there isn't as hard as some think. Getting there as a star is. In this segment we'll look at the various ways to get you in the position to hit your mark.

Auditioning Techniques

Be prepared long before the audition.
- Know your lines
- Get there early in case there were any changes to the sides you were given.
- Ignore the other actors. They'll try to throw you off your game. They're not your friends even if they are.

- Greet those auditioning you by looking them directly in the eyes while shaking their hands (firm shake of course; nobody likes limp) and repeat their names.
- Commit to character.
- Take direction without complaint.
- Thank them and don't steal anything on the way out.

On camera Techniques (maximizing your time on camera)

When I say maximize I really mean steal. Grab the attention of every scene you're in as long as it doesn't destroy the scene. You'll know you went too far if security has to become involved, but other than that here are a few scene stealing techniques to "maximize" your time on camera:

- Twist your ring
- Check your watch
- Stroke your hair
- Rub your nose
- Adjust your clothes
- Have your purse slip off your shoulder and pull it back up
- Place your palm at the back of your neck

The key is to always appear that your character is living a life within that scene. The person you're playing is not waiting to react to a line. The line almost interrupts what they were doing. Passive comedy performances are boring. Be active in every scene unless your character is dead.

Showcases

There are currently two types of showcases. One type of showcase gets you in front of industry representatives who can advance your career. The other gets you in front of other comics who will critique your set. Avoid the latter. It does not apply to this segment.

A showcase is exactly how it sounds. You get to showcase your talent. Make the most of it. Industry is going out to see live talent less and less. They're opting to view comedians from the comfort of their office and the clarity of their laptop. No 2 drink minimum. No parking hassles. No other comedians running up to them, putting in their bid. So if industry goes to all the trouble to show up you should do the same.

You're given a brief amount of time to make an impression. Go in there and blow them away. Leave it all on the stage. Give them no choice but to pick you for whatever it is. For showcases you want to step up your pace to get more into less time. The goal is to concentrate your laughs.

You want to have the same mindset for . . .

Competitions

Competitions do not validate you as a comedian. Winning does not make you better than everyone who did not. Winning competitions means you receive greater exposure. Winning competitions means you're rewarded financially. However, most of all winning competitions mean you know how to win competitions.

Like every other endeavor known to mankind there are little secrets those in the know utilize to gain an advantage over the pack.

The Ones to Enter to Help You

You don't have to enter every competition you hear about. Look for ones that advance your agenda.

Televised competitions are a double edged sword. It gives you access to millions you wouldn't have touched without that platform, but you have to shine. You don't have to win, but you do have to make an impression. If you do that you'll receive offers of work from commercials to touring to films and TV guest spots.

Techniques to Get Into the Winners Circle

Winning competitions is based on technique as well as comedic skill. It's also a matter of luck. Luck can't be controlled, but as you've learned throughout this manual, practiced techniques can.

The key to advancing in comedy competitions is to impress the judges by blowing away the audience from first phrase to last. Notice I said phrase not bit. The goal is to get a roll of laughter and the best way to do that is to overlap your laughs. Break the rule of not stepping on your punchlines and careen right over them. This will create a wall of sound and give the illusion of non-stop laughter (which in effect you will achieve if done properly). Get a laugh with every line of dialogue you utter. Snatch the mic from the stand when you grab it announcing to that audience that you're about to stampede into something powerful. You're about to unleash the beast they've been waiting to see all night. You're the one about to deliver that memorable set everybody will be talking about on the way home. Don't come up for air until you've said the last word. Leave the crowd exhausted and then get the standing ovation you deserve.

There is a technique to attaining standing ovations. Once you've hit your last punchline, lower your head, take a short, crisp bow and as you come up raise your arms to the side until they're above your head, then rise you head upward defiantly. It's bold and arrogant, but they will stand and the judges will give you a higher score.

The Tools of a Comedian

Getting work requires work. If you don't have a crack team of employees working on your behalf to get you gigs you have to do it yourself. You cannot rely on the referral of friends or the generosity of your local club owner to keep you in comedy. That requires hustling on your part. It means making calls, sending emails, networking in person and online. Join groups and have something to offer. Scratch backs, barter. Comedy is your job; treat it as such. Most jobs have a person work 8 hours a day. Why should comedy be any different? Nobody is suggesting you make calls for 8 hours a day, but think about the results you would get if you did. You'd have so much work you wouldn't have time to make calls.

However, let's not confuse stage time with work. Stage time is like a boxer working out in the gym. Work is an actual paying gig which is like the fight. You do stage time so you're ready for a gig. Your career is not a long line of only stage time. Your focus is to work and as much as possible.

Contracts

Every deal should be in writing. Every one that dictates that somebody put money in your hands for performing or providing any comedy service whatsoever. Without a valid agreement that person can claim its hearsay. It's your word against theirs what is owed. With a written agreement signed by both parties the one thing that can't be disputed is your fee. You're a professional (or at least trying to look like one) so do it right.

For simple gigs a deal memo will suffice.

For example:

PERFORMANCE AGREEMENT

This agreement is entered into on the xx day of Month 20xx, by Legal Name (hereinafter referred to as Promoter). The entertainer, **YOU** (hereinafter referred to as the **Entertainer**)

Venue of Performance: Name and Address

Date of Performance: Month xx, 20xx

Time of Performance: Whatever time it's supposed to start

PERFORMANCE FEES ARE AS FOLLOWS:
- The total booking fee are $1,000,000.00
- A non-refundable deposit of 50% ($500,000.00) is due immediately upon delivery of this agreement
- The balance of $500,000.00 is due upon the arrival of the **Entertainer** the day of the event
- Balance will be paid by cash, Paypal or a cashier's check. No personal checks.

PROMOTER'S RESPONSIBILITIES:
- **Promoter** will be responsible for all promotional advertisement pertaining to this event
- **Promoter** will provide a hotel room for **Entertainer** for the night of the event.
- **Promoter** will also provide a private closed off seating area, a complimentary meal and two drinks for the **Entertainer** upon arrival at the venue

ENTERTAINER'S RESPONSIBILITIES:
- The **Entertainer** will arrive at the venue on time for the performance
- The **Entertainer** will perform 45 minutes as agreed upon per the terms and conditions of the contract.
- The **Entertainer** will be responsible for the selling of his own merchandise after the show at the venue
- In the event of cancellation, the **Entertainer** must notify the client at least two weeks prior to the event and will accommodate the client with this matter in the event of cancellation

Your signature below confirms that all said parties have read and agree to the terms stated above.

Entertainer_____
Date _____
                        Signature

Promoter_____
Date _____
                        Signature

For more elaborate, detailed shows you'll want a full contract, such as;

PERSONAL APPEARANCE AGREEMENT

The signing of this Agreement by YOU (hereinafter "ARTIST"), and _____(hereinafter "PRESENTER") shall constitute a binding agreement between said parties. **Failure of either party to sign this Agreement shall automatically cancel the Agreement.**

FINANCIAL

1. Regarding the engagement of ARTIST on _____, for a fee of _____, the following terms and conditions shall apply.

2. A **50%** deposit shall be paid to ARTIST at signing to secure the date. Balance to be paid date of engagement.

3. ARTIST acknowledges that it is an independent contractor and not an employee of the PRESENTER. PRESENTER agrees to prepare and file all tax information required of a person who hires an independent contractor and the ARTIST agrees that they have the sole responsibility for payment of any federal and

state taxes arising from the monies paid by PRESENTER to the ARTIST for the Performance.

4. A copy of Form W-9 or Form W-8BEN is required from the ARTIST and its agent at the signing of this contract. Payment of performance fees cannot be made until a copy of the ARTIST's and its Agent's Form W-9 or Form W-8BEN are provided.

5. The price agreed upon is an all-inclusive fee, and no additional artist/hotel/transportation fees or charges will be paid.

TECHNICAL

6. Technical specifications should fall within the parameters of the technical specifications of PRESENTER'S facility unless otherwise mutually agreed.

7. Technical crew employed by PRESENTER shall report to and remain under direct supervision of PRESENTER at all times. ARTIST shall have control over artistic qualities of performance; however, PRESENTER shall control all non-artistic aspects of the venue's physical plant.

8. PRESENTER requests that the engagement length be at least 90 minutes in duration.

RECORDING, REPRODUCTION OR TRANMISSION OF PERFORMANCE

9. PRESENTER will make all reasonable efforts to prevent the recording, reproduction or transmission of the Engagement without the written permission of the ARTIST.

PUBLICITY AND PROGRAMS

10. Promotion, publicity, and advertising materials for publicizing this engagement, as called for by the Agreement, shall be furnished to the PRESENTER by the ARTIST as soon as possible.

11. PRESENTER respectfully requests that ARTIST shall make themselves reasonably available for telephone interviews with the local media, to be scheduled at mutually agreeable times.

12. PRESENTER retains exclusive rights over all advertising and promotion of the scheduled engagement but will discuss promotion with ARTIST. This is to include all paid ad buys, trade and sponsorship agreements through all media.

INSURANCE AND LIABILITY

13. If any actions by ARTIST or ARTIST'S employees, agents, or representatives are in conflict with any policies, rules or regulations of PRESENTER while ARTIST is on PRESENTER'S property, and ARTIST or its employees, agents, or representatives fail or refuse to correct within a commercially reasonable opportunity the same upon verbal notification by PRESENTER, then PRESENTER shall have the right to immediately terminate the Performance and cancel the Agreement with no liability whatsoever.

CANCELLATION

14. If the ARTIST does not perform due to cancellation by ARTIST for any reason other than Act Of God, PRESENTER shall be entitled to a refund of any and all

monies paid to ARTIST under this Agreement unless PRESENTER and ARTIST agree on a mutually acceptable date within the following twelve months to reschedule the ARTIST's performance.

15. In the event that the performance is likely to be rendered impossible, hazardous or otherwise prevented or impaired due to inclement weather, then PRESENTER and ARTIST will exercise all reasonable efforts to reschedule the performance.

MODIFICATION:

16. Any modification of this Agreement, or additional obligation assumed by either party in connection with this Agreement, shall be binding only if placed in writing and signed by each party or an authorized representative of each party.

FORCE MAJEURE

17. Neither the ARTIST nor PRESENTER shall be liable for failure to appear, present or perform if such failure is caused by or due to Acts Of God (e.g. fire, flood, blizzard, inclement weather, epidemic, or earthquake), the acts and regulations of public authorities, strike, civil tumult, war or act of terrorism, interruption or delay of transportation service, or any cause beyond the reasonable control of the ARTIST or PRESENTER, and is not caused by the negligence, intentional conduct or misconduct of the defaulting party, and the defaulting party has exercised all reasonable efforts to avoid or remedy such force majeure. The defaulting party must provide written notice of the force majeure event to the remaining parties within two (2) days of such event. ARTIST and PRESENTER will use their best efforts to reschedule performance for first mutually acceptable date.

SEVERABILITY

18. If any clause of this Agreement is judged to be invalid, such judgment does not affect the validity of the remaining clauses.

JURISDICTION/VENUE

19. The laws of the PRESENTER'S state shall govern all rights, obligations, remedies and liabilities arising pursuant to the Agreement. The ARTIST and PRESENTER agree that PRESENTER'S state shall be the venue for any disputes that may arise between ARTIST and PRESENTER.

FAXED & PDF SIGNATURES

20. Any document transmitted by facsimile machine or PDF scan shall be considered an original document and shall have the binding and legal effect of an original document. The signature of any party upon a document transmitted by facsimile shall be committed an original signature.

AGREED AND ACCEPTED:

_____

By PRESENTER

_____

(Print Name)

Date _____

_____
                                    by ARTIST

_____
                                    (Print Name)

Date _____

Whichever way you decide to go you should have a lawyer look over individual circumstances until the right agreement is tailored for you.

You should also have a rider. It spells out the various perks expected as part of the gig. You might require certain amenities in your hotel and/or dressing room. Pssst! This is where you can request the blue M&Ms be segregated from the other colors.

Negotiating Techniques

If you're contacting promoters yourself - keep the pitch simple:

"Hi (their name),

My name is (your name) and I'm a (feature / headlining) comedian scheduled to be in your area in (state a month or time frame). It would be great if we could schedule a booking during that time. Can I send over my material for you to review?"

This pitch makes an introduction, sets a time frame and requests a booking. It also answers some of your unspoken questions: If the promoter does not say they're all booked up during that time or they only book comedians they know, you're a possibility. If they provide you with their email for submission – this also lets you know you're a possibility, but more importantly they're giving you permission to call them back. When you do the follow-up pitch should be something like this:

"Hi (their name)
This is (your name). We spoke the other day and I submitted my materials to the email you gave me. Did you receive it?"

At this point the promoter has to answer that direct question. If not reconfirm the email, resubmit and run the same drill. If the promoter did receive it, you say . . .

"Good, glad you got it. What date(s) are best for a booking (names a date(s) or is (name another date(s) better?"

Assume the booking. Let the promoter tell you if they liked your material or not. Let the promoter tell you they never said they wanted to hire you. Let the promoter tell you neither of those time frames works for them. If they don't blurt out and say it when you ask if they received it assume they did and move things forward.

If the time frames you mentioned don't work for them mention you travel a lot. How does their schedule look the following season? Don't stop asking for a date (s) until they tell you yes or no.

Always highlight the benefit to the other person. Focus on all they'll receive for the modest price you're requesting. If it's a club owner let them know you sell drinks. You say, "Drink up" or "asks ""Does everybody have drink?" all throughout your act.

Referrals from other comedians (who were successful in that venue) always help. They can be part of a simple initial package that should include your bio/resume, a headshot and a link to your website or a set that represents your abilities. The set should be short (3-5 minutes), but impressive. If they want more they'll request it, but the reality is most promoters are not going to view your full 45 minutes. If so ask to be laid over another week. They love you.

Rule of thumb – ask for more than you expect to get, but sometimes you get a pleasant surprise and they say "sure". Negotiation over. However, when those rare instances happen don't get too curious. The ease of some talks might prompt you to feel gypped. You could've gotten more. How much more? Next thing you know you're asking them how much more. Now you look stupid and whatever answer they give you, the story of how you honestly asked after talks were completed is the story they'll tell for ages. You just became an anecdote.

At the end of an engagement always ask when you can return. If possible mark those future dates on the calendar along with the promoter right then and there.   Your price should be higher the next time, but if not it's still a booking and not a deal killer due to no raise.

Obtaining representation

The best way to get quality reps is to let them come to you. This can be done by a planned showcase or sheer luck they see you in a club or online.   However, if you're too impatient for serendipity, submit to talent agencies and management companies.   All the major unions have lists available.

Assembling a Motivated Team

A motivate team means they're out there working for you. It doesn't mean if something falls in their lap your team throws you a bone. You want an agent hustling gigs. You need a manager with judgment enough to guide your career in the right direction. You should have a publicist who knows all the little ins and outs of your industry and getting you mentioned every step of the way. Or you could bypass all of them and get a bad ass attorney.

Staying Relevant

One way to stay relevant is to be active. Do things your publicist can publicize. Keep your name out there. Collaborate, donate and appear at high profile photo ops (make sure you're in a shot with a celebrity. A picture of you alone will not make the Entertainment section) and keep them interested. Be part of the conversation. If you're shy to the point of resisting promoting your own interest comedy is not the route for you.

Stay relevant by staying interesting. Whether you're doing film, television, webisodes, radio, Internet radio, Satellite radio, online sketches, acting or a One Person Show - there are a variety of ways to carve a niche out for yourself. Write blogs, record vlogs, but whatever you do – stay in their faces with content.

Using Your Skills

In comedy there's no restriction on how you can express yourself. You can bring other talents to the game. Will Rogers, a cowboy as well as a comedian, would tell his jokes while doing tricks with a lasso. Many comedians, who are also musicians, sing and play instruments as part of their acts. Whatever you can incorporate naturally that adds to your stage persona should be used. In other words, if slopping hogs is one of your life skills . . . oh, never mind - you might want to pass on that one. Then again if you can make it funny . . .

In Conclusion

All professions set goals. Athletes, sales staffs, medical, legal, scientific – it doesn't matter the community of endeavor, everyone measures their progress or lack of by dangling a carrot. Comedy should be no different. If you're an opening act your goal should be to become a feature. A feature act should strive to become a headliner and headliners should want to become a headliner that other headliners fear. The point is to wake up each day with an agenda to follow.

Once you've decided what your ultimate goal in comedy is, setting goals to reach it should be relatively simple. For instance, if you've decided to become a comedy actor you need to work on your instrument which is you. Daily goals should be a workout regimen. You'll also need to work on your voice range and capability. Work on your education of your field by studying footage of great comedy actors and reading comedy scripts. Every single day you should do these things.

Your goals should be in increments. You should have daily, weekly, monthly, annual and long range (5 years- 10 years) goals. Perhaps you're reading a script a week; 4 scripts per month, etc. Maybe you've decided to audition a certain number of times monthly. Instead of New Year's resolutions you have New Year's career goals. How many TV shows do you want to appear on? How many films? If you don't have representation what is the target date to obtain it?

Deadlines are important in comedy. Don't feel hindered by them. You're only allowed a certain amount of time on stage. Why not view your advancement in the same fashion. Do you want to spend 10 years doing something that could've been done in five?

Goals help you avoid walking on the treadmill and making no progress. Comics do it all the time. You craft an act and beat it to death, week after week, year after year until one day you wake up and notice other acts have gone onto greater levels of success and you're still doing your act in the same clubs hoping to be discovered even though you live in Kentucky.

If you're going to make it in comedy you have to put yourself in the position to make it. If you do decide to concentrate on comedy acting, Community Theater is not your eventual win. You can hone your craft practically anywhere, but to show what you have and be on a horse even near the brass ring you need to be where those in your profession flourish. You don't want to wake up one day and realize you missed your window of opportunity because you never bought a bus or plane ticket to where the big time existed. So set goals that are realistic and those that stretch you as an artist and a person.

Money is important, but don't chase dollars. Chase a brand. Once you've established who you are as a talent the money comes along with your success. Ever hear of a successful person whining about money woes? The goal is to be a solid performer. You now have the tools to reach that end. Good luck in your career and consult this manual whenever the going gets rougher than you expect. So keep it handy.

Other Suggested Titles By Darryl Littleton

Available at Amazon.com and BN.com

CPSIA information can be obtained
at www.ICGtesting.com
Printed in the USA
LVHW081825231219
641488LV00037B/2113/P